Left Parties Everywhere?

Oskar Lafontaine

SPOKESMAN
for
SOCIALIST RENEWAL

Contents

Introduction   3
by Ken Coates

Left Parties Everywhere   5
An interview with Oskar Lafontaine

A New Left Party in France   9
by Oskar Lafontaine

Together for Change in Europe!   15
Platform of the Party of the European Left
for the elections to the European Parliament on 4 June 2009

Introduction
Ken Coates

2009 will be a year of slump and war. Large parts of the population of Europe feel themselves to be unrepresented as these dire developments unfold. There is clearly a wide vacuum in official politics, which has proved itself incapable of defending peace, jobs and democracy. But alternatives are beginning to emerge.

From its exciting beginnings in Germany, the movement to create Left Parties which can represent this fundamental disquiet about the effects of gathering slump, and official militarism, has been steadily advancing. Die Linke, the German Left Party, is led by Oskar Lafontaine, the SPD's candidate for Federal Chancellor in 1990, and Lothar Bisky, former Chairman of the Party of Democratic Socialism (PDS), which grew up in East Germany during the 1990s after the Berlin Wall came down. Die Linke has been advancing with phenomenal speed from one regional election to the next, entering the State Parliaments in Hesse and Hamburg in 2008. It is gaining membership and support continuously, with North Rhine Westphalia, Saarland, Lower Saxony, and Bavaria registering particularly strong growth in recent times. Its Federal Parliamentary group includes 54 deputies, making it the fourth largest in the Bundestag.

Now there has been an initiative in France to create an answering response to developments in Germany, with the formation of a new Party of the Left (Parti de Gauche). Three thousand people joined in the founding conference in Paris, and already they have some presence in sixty different *départements*. This pamphlet includes the speech by Oskar Lafontaine to that founding meeting, together with an article published in *Spokesman* No. 100, under the title *Left Parties Everywhere*.

Left Parties are now appearing all over the place. In Greece, Syriza, a federation led by Alecos Alavanos won fourteen seats in the Greek General Election of 2007, and has gathered substantial support among young people. In Portugal and the Netherlands strong Left Parties are already establishing themselves. These and similar developments will give especial importance to the European Elections which are to be held in June 2009. What will be the response of the British Left to these developments?

Of course, it takes time to form a new Party from the fragments of old struggles. The French, and the Germans, have both built their alliance from movements within the old political system. It is hard to foretell what will happen in the British Labour Party as the slump gathers its crushing momentum, and the effects of past and continuing wars continue to shock large numbers of people.

An important presence on the British Left already exists in the Green Party, led by Caroline Lucas, the MEP from the South East Constituency. Jean Lambert, her colleague from London, will also be standing in the European Elections in June, and there are a number of other Green candidates who must be counted as possible victors in the complex ballots that must take place on June 4.

Is it possible that those who might already wish to form Left Parties* in England, Wales and Scotland could negotiate with the Greens about common policies and joint actions? Would this not be a valuable preparation for the situation that will emerge, as the Labour Party enters the crisis it is likely to experience in the fraught developing age of slump and war?

*We would, of course, very much like to hear from those who are interested in this proposal.

Ken Coates was for the last two years of his Parliamentary term a member of the United Left Group in the European Parliament.

Left Parties Everywhere
Oskar Lafontaine

Oskar Lafontaine served as Prime Minister of Saarland and President of the German Bundesrat. He was the SPD's candidate for Federal Chancellor in 1990, when he was attacked and critically wounded with a knife. In September 1998, he was appointed Federal Minister of Finance, and resigned the following March. In 2005, he left the SPD and founded the Left Party, which subsequently merged with the PDS, the successor to the Socialist Unity Party of Germany (SED) in the German Democratic Republic. Lafontaine is now joint Chairman of the merged Left Party (Die Linke). In September 2008, he gave an interview to the newspaper Neues Deutschland, from which we reprint excerpts. The questions are in italic text and Mr Lafontaine's replies in ordinary type.

* * *

Mr Lafontaine, since Die Linke was founded, not even so much as an historic blink of the eye has elapsed, and already the party has moved into four state assemblies in the West of Germany. It is on the point of becoming an all-German party, maybe even an all-German catch-all party. Did you think this success possible?

Two years ago I would not have thought that we could be so successful so quickly. Yet, apparently more and more people want politics in Germany to change. The policy of the governing grand coalition is marked by value added tax fraud, social decline, increasing the retirement age to 67, and involvement in wars in defiance of international law. The majority of people refuse this and see in Die Linke a new political force that counters it.

SPD Chair Kurt Beck [who has since resigned] said your party was an adversary. Is the SPD also an adversary to you?

Of course. Parties compete for voters. And in this respect the SPD is an adverse party, like other parties, too. Naturally, as the example of Hesse shows, there are overlapping features in the programmes of the SPD and Die Linke. After the elections, it would be natural for all parties involved to sit down together on the basis of what they said in their programmes and ask: where is the common ground and what is the best way to co-operate? The parties competing with us are not that mature at the moment.

Do you think Kurt Beck's course has a future in the SPD? Does the SPD have a future pursuing this course?

Originally Beck stood for a strategy that had to fail. It was that you can co-operate with Die Linke in the East but not in the West. It was certain that this strategy would not last. He has now corrected this mistake. Now we have to wait to see how things develop. Die Linke adheres to its fundamental statement: we want to change politics. And we are ready to co-operate with others on the basis of our programme.

Your party is accused of living in cloud-cuckoo-land: your programme is not financially affordable.

I only have to say one sentence: not a single cut in welfare services would have been necessary in the past few years if we had the average European tax rate, which is about 40%. Ours is 35%. I promised each journalist, each professor and each politician a gold watch if they managed to refute that statement. So far I have not yet had to give away any gold watches; that means the objections of our adversaries are wrong, knowing the figures ...

Quite often it is questioned that you are on the left. Are you?

What is left? I have a simple answer: Left is when you side with the employees, the pensioners, and the socially needy, when in doubt. That is what we do. And I do, too.

Cue 25 April 1990. Do you still remember that day? Do you dream about it?

That was the day an attempt was made on my life. That was 18 years ago, and I think I have come to grips with it to a large degree. During the first years, it kept me more on my toes. What was decisive for me was that I recognised one always has to live in a way so one can say I did things right, because tomorrow life can be over.

Do you manage?

When it comes to my own demands and yardsticks, yes. It is important to me that you should treat people the way you would like

to be treated yourself. This is also a short programme for Die Linke.
Nevertheless, your life is inseparably linked to social democracy, is it not? In 1985, you became the first Social Democratic Prime Minister of the Saarland, and in 1990 you ran for Chancellor. In 1995 you were elected party chair. Does your heart still beat for the SPD, the SPD as it once was? Or have you found a new political home in Die Linke, which you co-founded?

When it comes to the SPD, membership always meant commitment to programmes and political ideas. The party was not a club such as a choir or sports club, but rather an association used to achieve political goals. Willy Brandt described one pivotal goal: peace. When he received the Nobel Peace Prize he called war the *ultima irratio* in his speech. These days the SPD again says war is the *ultima ratio*. I stick with Willy Brandt's sentence: war is the *ultima irratio*. My heart still beats for this sentence.
On the other hand, I have a hand in founding Die Linke. It takes a lot of work, heart and soul. Die Linke is my political home now. It is already about to change German politics, and this is very important to us.

Why do you think today's SPD has veered so far away from Willy Brandt's SPD?

The heart of the matter for the Left is to what extent does it manage not to fall for the temptations and seductions of capitalist power structures? The SPD did not manage to do so, resulting in leading social democratic politicians ending up with some private equity firms or major gas consortiums. Still, some decades ago this would have been unimaginable. Brandt and Wehner in a private equity firm or temporary employment company? Unthinkable ...

What is your goal? Do you want to unite both parties, Die Linke and the SPD, one day?

This question is often raised. Yet, the SPD and Die Linke are completely different. Without a doubt there is only time for one thing: German politics needs a left party. Not only German politics, but also European politics, because the formerly socialist and social democratic parties have been pocketed by neoliberalism over the past few years. If you want social renewal, you need new left parties everywhere. Nothing can grow together that does not belong together.

You once said Die Linke now stood for the SPD programme which had still met with much approval from the voters in 1989. You were head of the commission then, which drew up the social democratic principles that are known as the Berlin programme. Almost 20 years have passed. Is this programme still timely? Do programmes not have to change, inevitably?

Yes and no. If the programme includes giving employees and pensioners a decent share of the increase in prosperity, this is timeless. The same applies to the pension formula that avoids poverty in old age. And saying that we need a foreign policy that respects international law, and never gets involved in wars in defiance of international law, as was the basis for the SPD programme in the times of Willy Brandt, this is timeless as well. Sometimes it is really aggravating to see that such principles are treated as if they are no longer modern. There are programme principles of Die Linke that are as constant as the guarantee of human rights by the Basic Law (constitution). Yet, certainly each time needs its new answers. Let's take the discussion on the general strike or mass strike, which Die Linke has triggered in Germany. Such positions were neither discussed by the SPD nor the Socialist Unity Party of Germany (SED) in the past. And talking about an ecological renewal today, and making re-municipalising a programme principle of Die Linke, and noting with surprise that other parties pick up on the subject of re-municipalising energy suppliers, this is very much an answer of the present time. Thirty or forty years ago, energy supply was still a municipal business. Later it was more and more privatised. Now we say that step was wrong and correct it. It stands out particularly in this place how thoughtless the argument is that you cannot suggest anything that used to exist some time ago …

Once again about your election successes, you personally are said to be for involvement in government. Is that true?

That always makes me laugh because, when you add up all the times, I probably was in government longest in Germany, including the time as Mayor of Saarbrücken. My position is clear. If you can accomplish your own policies, you have to enter government. If not, you must try to do so in opposition. We, Die Linke, are particular proof of the fact that a relatively small political force can change politics as an opposition party.

A New Left Party in France

Oskar Lafontaine

The joint Chair of Die Linke spoke in Paris on 29 November 2008 at the launch of Parti de Gauche.

Ladies, Gentlemen, Dear Comrades!

It is with pleasure that I have come to Paris to speak to you about building in France a new party of the left which truly merits the name. In Germany we have done this with some success. And it is with the strength of this experience that I come here to encourage you to take the same path. I know very well that the constellation of German political parties is not comparable to the French situation. But today, French and German society do not differ fundamentally from one another. The economic, political and social problems which our countries face are largely identical. I do not see any major reason why a new party of the left shouldn't have the same chances of success in France as in Germany.

Now that Die Linke (The Left) has existed for a year and a half, the serious polls give it 12 to 13% support at the national level. I must tell you that I am surprised myself at this success. Because these figures do not measure the full breadth of our political influence – the fact that we are there, the fact that there exists in Germany a party with a political profile and social demands clearly of the left: this has changed the orientation of German politics. We are not alone in saying this. Almost all the German newspapers say the same, whether they are of the right or left, whether they rejoice in or deplore the fact. For the most part, they are of one accord that we, the party 'Die Linke', are the most successful political project of recent decades, that we increasingly define the political agenda in Germany, that we push the other parties to react. If they react, if they adopt certain social demands, this is because they fear the voters. And if neoliberalism, so virulent since 1990, is in the process of disappearing in Germany, that is due in good part to our parliamentary presence.

Dear Comrades, it is evident that the constitution of a new party of the left could not succeed if the external conditions, that is to say the social and political situation in Germany, hadn't been favourable to the project. That is the first criterion of success. But because all the West German political parties dispute the 'centre' and advocate a neoliberal economic policy, a majority of the German population deplore the resulting lack of social equilibrium. The empty space on the left of the political spectrum demands to be filled. There is nothing more potent than an idea whose time has come.

The second criterion of success is, without doubt, the union of forces and political organisations which define themselves by a critical position towards capitalism.

The third criterion, which is perhaps the easiest to realise, although this doesn't depend on us alone, but is no less important, is to give the new party a clear profile, sharply discernible in comparison with the uniformity of the others. I do not seek to define this third point more precisely by what follows, but I would like to approach it by an historical observation. It is sometimes useful to step back a little to have a better view of the whole.

At the beginning of my political career, some forty years ago, the positions of the parties of the left in Europe were relatively clear, their missions well defined. There was not the centrist uniformity of which the big parties make a show nowadays. Even in Germany, where the Social Democrats, at Bad Godesberg, had decided to make an accommodation with capitalism, left and right remained distinguishable to the voters. The SPD detached itself from Marxism, most certainly, but retained the idea of reforming capitalism all the same; of finding the famous 'third way' between communism and capitalism. Unfortunately, this reformist ideal has been buried under the debris of the Berlin Wall.

In France, the position of the parties of the left was even clearer – not only on the communist side, but also on the part of the socialists. Because of its support for the colonial war in Algeria, the SFIO had lost, by the end of the 1960s, all legitimacy as a party of the left. In 1971, at the Epinay Congress, a new socialist party formed itself under the direction of François Mitterrand. The programme of this new French socialist party differed considerably from that which the German Social Democrats had set out a good decade before: it was anti-capitalist, it was critical of NATO, and favourable to alliances with the Communist Party – everything that the SPD programme wasn't.

It was Epinay versus Godesberg within the Socialist International. I'm German, but I do not hide from you that my sympathies were with Epinay.

I shared then, dear comrades, your disappointments. Because in spite of this theoretically anti-capitalist programme, the practical policy of the Mitterrand Government was scarcely more anti-capitalist than that of the Social Democratic government in Germany. For there was in England, in Germany, in Spain, in France and elsewhere a gap between theory and practical policy that is symptomatic of the history of West European socialism. Almost always and almost everywhere, the rulers of these socialist parties dropped their principles – often against the wishes of the mass of militants – for a government portfolio.

And this is exactly the big dilemma of these socialist parties: to formulate the principles of opposition at Epinay, and the principles of government at Godesberg. The history of West European socialist parties in power is a long list of rotten compromises. Dear comrades, we must leave behind this dilemma, and break with this fatal tradition of rotten compromises. For a party of the left, the principles of government must always be the same as the principles of opposition. If not, it will disappear more quickly than it arrived.

Look at Italy, look at Spain! The lesson the left must draw from the most-recent elections in those countries couldn't be clearer: IU marginalized in Spain, Rifondazione Comunista eliminated in Italy. These two parties have paid very dearly for their participation in government because it was based on rotten compromises. It is an absurdity, in effect, to quit a party because of its political line, in order to construct a new party, only to go on to form a governmental coalition with that party which you have just left, on the basis of the same policy which caused you to leave in the first place. The voters scarcely appreciate this kind of trick – and they're not wrong.

Dear friends, if the left loses its credibility, it loses its *raison d'être*. It is for this reason that my party, Die Linke, has taken steps to impede the rulers' fatal tendency to compromise, of which I have just spoken. Decisions on the major principles of our programme must be taken by the militants of the party all together, and not only by an assembly of delegates. Besides, we do not accept donations above a certain level, which is relatively low. And believe me, it is not the attitude of the fox who sees the grapes are out of reach, which is responsible for this self-denying ordnance. This is simply because we do not want to be corrupted. Political corruption is the scourge of our time. And the so-called 'donation' is often a legal means of corruption. The electoral victory of Barack Obama is good news, to the extent that the policy of President Bush and his party didn't find support. But looking at the enormous sums which American capital has invested in the electoral campaign of the new president, I remain very sceptical about his future momentum of reform. Capital never gives without taking.

We come now to the programmatic profile that a party of the left must have, in my opinion. I say straightaway that my sympathies, for almost forty years, have been on the side of Epinay, and not Godesberg. Ah well, it was always thus. Now, perhaps, more than ever. The anti-capitalist spirit, which animated the French left in the 1970s, asserted itself always. Certainly, a manipulated public opinion at the service of capital relayed across all media was told that globalisation would completely change these choices, that anti-capitalism had passed into history. But if one analyses dispassionately the economic and social processes which are unfolding before our eyes, one realises that globalisation has not dissipated but aggravated the social problems and the economic turbulence caused by capitalism. If you compare Marx's writings on the concentration of capital, imperialism or the internationalisation of finance capital with the neoliberal follies put around in our time, you notice that the 19th century author is more precise and prescient than the ideologues of fashionable neoliberalism.

Dear friends, more than ever anti-capitalism is at stake, because imperialism, at the beginning of the 21st century, remains entirely real. And NATO is instrumental in its service. Long ago conceived as a defensive alliance, in our time NATO has become an alliance of intervention under the direction of the United States. But the left cannot advocate a foreign policy which has as its objective the military conquest of resources and markets. We do not accept NATO's belligerent imperialism, which intervenes throughout the world, contrary to international law. We are for a system of collective security where the partners support each other reciprocally if they are attacked, but abstain from all violence which does not conform to international law.

In Germany, the question of military intervention – whether it was about Kosovo, or is about Afghanistan – is a line of clear demarcation between my party, Die Linke, and all the other parties, including the Social Democrats. We are intransigent on this point, and our participation is inconceivable in a government favourable to NATO military intervention. The question of war and peace, more than ever, has at all times been a reason for schism at the heart of German socialism. Already in 1916 – under the impulse of Rosa Luxemburg and Karl Leibknecht – the war had divided German social democracy into two parts. And it wasn't only in Germany that the left had a clear view. I remind you of the calls of Jean Jaurès that 'capitalism carries war within itself, as storm clouds carry the storm'. Comrades, if we want a world of peace, we must civilise capitalism.

Contrary to the ideology of privatisation preached by the spokesmen of neoliberalism, we safeguard the idea of a public economy under democratic control. We advocate a mixed economy where private enterprises, by far the majority, exist side by side with nationalised enterprises. Above all, enterprises which meet society's fundamental needs of existence – the energy sector, for example, or the banking sector insofar as it is indispensable to the functioning of all the economy – must be nationalised.

We restore to the agenda the questions of workers' control and employee participation in decisions about the capital of their enterprises, which seem to have been forgotten nowadays.

We struggle against a policy of social dismantling which gives priority to investors' interests and scoffs at increasing social injustice, at the poverty of many children, low salaries, redundancies in the public services, at the destruction of the eco-system. We struggle against a policy which sacrifices the demands of public opinion to the returns on finance capital. We do not accept the privatisation of social security systems, nor that of public transport. Nor do we accept the further privatisation of the energy sector, and even more so, the privatisation of public education and culture. Our fiscal policy seeks to restore to the state the means to fulfil its classical functions.

Today, the motor forces of capitalism are no longer the entrepreneurs, but rather the financial investors. It is finance capitalism which governs the world, and installs the casino economy globally. The crisis of the financial markets was foreseeable, awaited by the experts. However, the governments did nothing to avert this crisis. In the United States and Great Britain, the political élites judged uncontrolled speculation to be useful. Continental Europe is inclined against this judgement. Yet no corrective measure has been taken during these times when the majority of European governments were formed by parties affiliated to the Socialist International. A critical dimension with respect to capitalism has been lamentably absent in the opportunistic policy embraced by socialist and social democratic parties all along the line. If proof of this failure is needed, then the current crisis of the financial markets delivers it.

And if there must be a proof that we, the critical left, are not regressive, that we do not use old remedies against today's ills, as the liberals and conservatives constantly reproach us, if proof is needed, this crisis delivers it also. Since the beginning of the 1990s, and the globalisation that followed, the left, and I include myself in its number, never ceased to demand regulation of international financial markets. But the neoliberals rejected what they called 'regressive' opinions. The logic of globalisation was not compatible with regulation, they told us; above all, we must not impede free exchange and free movement of capital transnationally, they preached to us; all regulation is outdated, regressive.

And now, what are the neoliberals in North America and England doing, what are the conservatives in Germany and France doing? Ah well – they pretend to regulate. Those who accused us of political regression when we demanded the nationalisation of certain banking sectors to avoid crisis, what are they doing now? They are pretending to nationalise the banks for the sake of the future.

Now the losses are socialised and the most vulnerable groups in society must pay for the failure of the system. Pompous international summits are organised to regulate the financial markets. But we are not dupes: the elephants are going to give birth to a mouse. Are they going to close the casino? Don't even think of it! Are they going to radically change the rules of play inside the casino? No! What they are going to do is to elaborate, with great fanfare, a new code of conduct for the croupiers. Nothing is really going to change.

If you want changes, comrades, it is necessary to reconstruct the left – in Germany, in France, all over Europe. The German experience shows us that a European left, reorganised and strong, can change the choices and force the other parties to react. Let us build this new left together, a left that refuses rotten compromises! To underline for the last time the importance of this maxim, I finish with an image borrowed from the Russian poet Mayakovsky:

Let's sing together,
but don't let's strangle our own song.

Translated by Tony Simpson

Together for Change in Europe!
*21ˢᵗ Century Europe needs
peace, democracy, social justice and solidarity*
**Platform of the Party of the European Left
for the elections to the European Parliament 2009**

I

The elections to the European Parliament in June 2009 will be an opportunity to change the European Union's foundations, and open a new perspective for Europe.

We face a financial, economic and social crisis, a crisis of the whole system, which is growing day by day. It increases and worsens the food, energy and ecological crises. It deepens the gender gap. It has a direct impact on the lives of all people in Europe and the world. Everywhere in the European Union the shock is tremendous. The crisis is caused by neoliberal globalised capitalism: namely, the irresponsible political and economic élites who pushed ahead with this hazardous capitalism, the price of which is being paid by the people. It endangers peace, international security and coexistence. The world has been led into this global crisis by the hegemonic policy of the United States, in particular that of the Bush administration.

The crisis once again demonstrates the failure of neoliberal globalisation, which has maximised profits of the financial markets' main players on a global scale without any state control or intervention. Politics, states and entire societies are subordinated to uncontrolled financial markets. The result is clear: a lack of democracy, and an end to the welfare state.

Low wages and precarious jobs, which are the consequences of deflationary measures applied by governments in developed countries, have put the financial and credit system at risk.

Governments, European Union institutions and world economic bodies such as the International Monetary Fund, the World Bank, and the World Trade Organisation have imposed privatisation and deregulation.

As a result, the neoliberal foundations of European Union treaties are called into question, in particular, the insistence on an 'open market economy with free competition', the unchecked and free circulation of capital, the liberalisation and privatisation of public services, and the status and mission of the European Central Bank.

This historic crisis strikes at the heart of capitalism. It challenges us to contribute to the resistance of the people, and to open a perspective for change in Europe. The Party of the European Left believes that a way out of this crisis can only be found by fighting for a democratic and social Europe: 'A Europe of the people, not of the banks'.

This is also a political crisis. The Irish, French and Dutch noes to the Lisbon and European Constitutional Treaties have shown that an increasing number of people in Europe disagree with the undemocratic and unsocial policies of the European Union. They believe the EU is a remote and incomprehensible construction which does not concern them, and ignores their hopes and their actual situation.

We reaffirm our No to the Lisbon Treaty. The democratic expression of the people's will must be respected within a new democratic process, based on active participation by the people and the national and European parliaments. Democratic participation and parliaments' powers must be strengthened through norms on popular petitions, co-decision enlargement, and the relations between national parliaments and the European Parliament. European Union citizens need to discuss and decide on an alternative to the Lisbon Treaty.

The European Union interferes in the lives of the people of Europe. Fifteen years after the Maastricht Treaty, neoliberal orientations prevail: the living and working conditions of the majority of Europe's population have rapidly worsened – longer working hours, longer working lives, insufficient wages, growing long-term and youth unemployment, mini jobs, temporary employment, and unpaid internships are all scandalous realities. By and large, public services are used for profit. Along with this come psychological and physical pressure, diseases, fear, loss of solidarity, and violence against the weaker elements in society. The situation of migrants in the European Union and its member countries, as well as EU migration policy, dramatically reflect this. On the other hand, profits have increased tremendously: senior managers receive astronomical salaries, even when their actions have negative consequences. The rich are getting richer, and the poor are growing poorer.

With regard to recent events in Europe, such as the Caucasus conflict, developments in Kosovo, bilateral treaties with the United States on the construction of US military bases in Eastern Europe, and the on-going arms race, it is important for the European Union to respect international law, and to find political solutions to any conflict.

The militarisation of European Union foreign policy linked to NATO must be replaced by an alternative concept of security based on peace, dialogue and international co-operation.

Many people are disappointed with, frustrated by, or turning away from European politics. Others are struggling for their jobs and social security, for public services, and the right to participate in political decision-making. They fight for their political, social and individual rights, for respect of human rights of all people living in the European Union. Migration and asylum have become an urgent issue in the political struggle. People strive for gender equality and democracy, justice and the right of all people to live in dignity and solidarity with each other.

More than ever the European Union is at a crossroads:
- either it continues its current capitalist policy, which is deepening its financial, security, food and energy crisis;
- or the European Union becomes an area of sustainable development and social justice, of peace and mutual cooperation, of equality of women and men, of democratic participation and solidarity, where anti-fascism, anti-racism, civil liberties and human rights are common practice.

The choice is in the hands of the people. To overcome resignation or abstention, we say alternatives exist. Policies both at the national and the European levels must and can be changed.

The European Left demands that this Europe must be a peaceful and civil Europe, where economies are socially and ecologically sustainable, that is feminist, and develops on the basis of democracy and solidarity. This needs a new synergy between social and political forces. It requires ideas, initiatives and the hard work of political actors and democratic forces, of trade unions and social movements, of representatives of civil societies. Alternatives are possible – through common struggle, both in the streets and in the parliaments.

We join the struggle of the peace and anti-war movement, of the anti-globalization movement, of all those resisting precarious living, the struggles of workers, women and youth.

Together with the representatives of other socialist, communist and Nordic left-green parties, we have successfully co-operated within the United European Left/Nordic Green Left (GUE/NGL) group in the European Parliament. The pluralistic character of this group has enriched the creative power of the left opposition between 2004 and 2009. We want to develop further this experience in the European Parliament to be elected in June 2009.

In light of the current crisis, the European Left is all the more called on to play an effective role in bringing about common political action against the political and cultural hegemony of the Right.

Neoliberal policies in the European Union were possible, among other reasons, because of a kind of grand coalition between the parties of the European Conservative forces and the European Socialists. This consensus is one of the reasons for a political crisis in the way Europe functions. It creates big contradictions inside the Social Democratic parties.

The European Left competes against conservative, liberal, social democratic and green parties in the member countries, and with the corresponding European political parties, which are sticking to the logic of current European policies. The European Left is striving for change and regaining the political space in Europe.

The European Left confirms its continuing struggle against any attempt by extreme right and right-populist parties to broaden their influence in Europe.

II
Overcome the Crisis: People before Profits
For a Social and Ecological Economy in Europe

The crisis demands a co-ordinated answer at the international and European levels.

The European Left stands for a policy that is based on economic and social development and the protection of the environment. It aims at the defence and development of social achievements.

Contrary to the Lisbon strategy, we strive for a strategy sustained on the values of solidarity and co-operation, full employment, and a rational relationship with nature. This is possible only by changing the existing rules of the international economic and financial system.

It is necessary to re-found the European Union on the basis of new parameters, able to focus on people and rights before profits.

We stress that the workers should not have to pay for the crisis while banks and finances are saved. The logic of the G7's plans for the European Union means privatising the profits and socialising the losses.

However, even current legislation allows expenditure on an investment plan to sustain employment, and to support ecological restructuring of the economy.

In matters of finance, the crisis has made obvious the determining part taken by credit. Credit must be redirected to the productive sectors of the economy and the collectivities, to employment, social and environmental priorities. This must be done all the way from the cities and regions to the European Central Bank System. To realise this reorientation of credit and money, we stand for public and social control of the banking and financial system. We stand for the right of working people and their organisations, as well as locally elected people, to control the use of credits and subsidies.

We criticise the aims and current policies of the European Central Bank: its absolute independence from any form of political accountability; the lack of transparency in its decisions and actions. We underline the urgent necessity that its monetary policy must respond to goals of new economic and employment growth, which are priorities with regards to inflation maintenance.

Therefore, the European Central Bank's role must be changed, in line with criteria of employment, and social and ecological development, by a selective decrease of interest rates. The Bank must submit to public and democratic control. It statutes must be changed.

The Growth and Stability Pact must be replaced by a new solidarity pact focusing on growth, full employment, and social and environmental protection.

We need to tax financial transactions and income in Europe, and abolish tax havens. It is also necessary to introduce taxation of speculative capital in order to feed the creation of a European Fund.

Capital movements, in particular profits that are not directly linked with investment and trade, must be subject to control and taxation.

The Tobin Tax can be the tool to finance innovative industrial initiatives in the sectors indicated by international UN agencies, and aimed at reducing global emissions and increasing the number of jobs. This European Fund would have to be submitted to the European Parliament's guidelines and programmes: a sort of 'new green deal' of the Parliament itself.

The common goods and economically strategic sectors, including the credit and financial system, must be socialised (nationalised), while there is also the need to rebuild a general welfare system on a European scale. The privatisation of public services must be reversed. We need to raise workers' wages and incomes. We need to harmonise the European financial system, based on the principle of progressive taxation.

As for new rights and powers of employees and citizens, they should enable them to break the monopoly of strategic information and decisions held by the main players in the market, and claim them for themselves in order to achieve a real transformation of political power. Democracy must begin with the involvement of the citizens themselves, and must be extended to every sphere of social life.

Sustainable European standards preventing poverty should replace the current policy of wage, social and environmental dumping. As the rulings of the European Court of Justice represent strong attacks on collective agreements and labour regulations, we stress the necessity to strengthen collective agreements and reinforce workers' rights. We reject the EU directive that extends working time up to 65 hours per week, allowing total flexibility, and boosting individualisation of work. For us, maximum weekly working hours permitted by law must, on average, not exceed 40 hours. All European Union regulations and national laws on working hours must be changed accordingly. We struggle for 35 hours per week on a Europe-wide basis. Where there exist better national regulations, they should be preserved. We demand a European minimum wage that represents at least 60% of the national average wage, and does not put at risk collective agreements.

A minimum income for unemployed people, as well as a minimum pension linked to the minimum wage which is automatically adjusted for inflation, is necessary to guarantee a life of dignity. Flexible retirement ages should be guaranteed, taking into account existing regulations in European Union member countries.

We demand a strengthening of migrants' rights to work wherever they live in the European Union. Migration law should focus on migrants' interests, and not on the interests of companies that are looking for cheap labour, which forces millions of migrants to work in the black market. We reject any regulation or directive in the European Union and its member countries imposing expulsion. What is needed is regulation and a work permit for employment research.

We reject the Lisbon concept of 'Flexicurity'. Our priorities are the steps against poverty, social marginalisation and precariousness, for full employment in regular jobs, and increasing wages, pensions and social allowances. Taxes must be raised both on income and capital, allowing redistribution from the top to the bottom.

Education, child care, care during adolescence, illness and old age, health, water supply and sewage disposal, energy supply, public transport, postal services, culture and mass sport are not commercial goods but public services that form part of the state's responsibilities. Therefore, they must not be subject to competition for the lowest costs and highest profits. We want no more privatisation of public services and goods, but a reversal or conversion into public property. We are for strong public services, publicly controlled companies, and more investment in education, nursing and health care, public transport, culture and sport.

For us climate and social questions are linked. Therefore, the current financial and economic crises cannot be separated from the challenges of climate change, and a reorientation of our ways of production and consumption. We are in favour of the immediate and consistent development of a new international treaty in accordance with the fourth report of the Intergovernmental Panel on Climate Change, and sticking to the EU action plan 2007-2009. We demand the full implementation of the signed and promised obligations of the European Union in all fields of climate and energy policies. The following compromises represent the minimum for the implementation of all climate protection commitments already signed:

- Reduce global emissions by 30% by 2020 on the exit level of 1990, and by at least 80% by 2050.
- Increase the use of renewable energy by at least 25% by 2020.
- Reduce total primary energy consumption by 25% by 2020, and increase energy efficiency by two per cent per year, including a limit on per capita consumption.

- An efficiency obligation needs to be introduced for industry and the producers of energy-intensive goods.
- EU framework subsidies are to be limited, consequently, to the energy efficiency and renewable energies sectors.

We are against reducing the Kyoto Protocol to a market system of quota emissions. It is necessary, in order to conclude the Kyoto 2 treaty, to have a new comprehensive strategy that allows the reduction of emissions making the development fairer and more sober. A new paradigm based on co-operation, instead of competition, is needed, starting with technology transfer to developing countries, the funding of clean technologies, and policies of adjustment to climate change.

Water is a universal good and the access to it must be guaranteed as a human right.

The protection of nature and the development of renewable resources, the transformation of our landscapes, as well as secure food supply are all existential challenges. We demand agreement on the highest environmental standards within the European Union, and contributions to saving biodiversity for future generations (active steps for waste reduction, water protection, for replanting and desertification prevention policies, and so on must be included in strategies and policies, in particular in the fields of agriculture, energy and climate protection).

We strive for a substantial review of the EU Common Agricultural Policy (CAP). It must be directed at the right of people everywhere in the world to decide on their agricultural policy themselves by fully respecting the environment.

We oppose any reform of the Common Agricultural Policy that challenges public agricultural policies. We demand that agriculture must not be a matter for World Trade Organistion negotiations, and oppose agriculture becoming more and more a playground for neoliberal actors and liberalisation measures worldwide. We support the request for food sovereignty.

This means giving priority to local agricultural production, quality food, and no constraints on submitting products to the world market. The access to land, seeds, water and credits must be regulated in a real land reform in Europe and the other continents.

We demand a comprehensive rural development policy: the development of agricultural production and employment opportunities should constitute the central criteria of the development of the countryside, with the application of sector-based policies, support of agricultural biodiversity and rural employment, particularly for young people and women. Subsidies should be given with economic, social and environmental criteria, and not for the profit of big producers in certain sectors. Starting from that point, the distribution of the Common Agricultural Policy budget must be re-oriented, in particular to the needs of rural areas, small-scale producers, disadvantaged and mountainous areas.

Agriculture in the 21st century must correspond to a multifunctional aspect: protection of plant multiplicative material, guaranteeing the right of farmers to have their own seeds, applying programmes of development of organic agriculture and livestock farming, and prohibiting the use of 'genetically modified organisms' (GMO) in the production of foods and foodstuffs, defending and valorising denomination origin also in non-European markets.

III
A peaceful and co-operative Europe

No war should ever start on Europe's soil again. We do not consider war and militarisation to be political instruments, and seek a strategy where security for all is granted.

Disarmament and the conversion of military industries are pivotal tasks. We campaign against the rearmament provision of the Lisbon Treaty, not only because of lethal and ecologically destructive weapons, but also because it detracts funds from economic, social and ecological development. The European Union Defence Agency should be replaced by a disarmament agency, designed to stop the arms race, proliferation and possession of weapons of mass destruction, as well as the militarisation of outer space and the oceans, on the basis of disarmament agreements.

Emerging conflicts on the European continent – in particular, after the refusal by governments to rethink co-operation of all European states on a just and equal basis since 1990 – point up the necessity of creating a new collective security system on the European continent. From a regional crisis to a war situation, the Caucasus conflict, in August 2008, eventually became an international crisis that now involves the United States. We call on civil society in Europe and the European Union to strive for a political solution. The danger of such conflicts spreading into other European regions remains of topical relevance. At the same time, the deployment of NATO forces in

Afghanistan, and growing demands from the US administration to increase European participation there, shows the failure of the military intervention strategy followed by the Bush administration. It demonstrates a growing contradiction between European interest in security and the military intervention strategy together with NATO expansion.

The European Left reaffirms its demand for the dissolution of NATO. We oppose the logic of military blocs, including attempts and policies for creating European military structures.

More than ever, security in Europe must be based on the principles of peace and security, disarmament and structural assault incapacity, conflict solution by political and civil means within the system of the Organisation for Security and Co-operation in Europe, conforming to international law and to the principles of a reformed and democratised UN system. Such a collective and co-operative European system must guarantee security and unconditional access to energy supply, environmental and human rights issues, and so on.

We need to stress the politically, and not only militarily, negative role that NATO plays according to US interests in Europe. Even after the end of East-West bloc confrontation, NATO remained. It was developed into an even more functional tool of US administrations for their hegemonic strategies. The NATO enlargement to the East corresponds to this logic.

The bilateral agreements of the United States with various European countries, such as the ones with Italy for the Vicenza US military base, with Poland and the Czech Republic for deploying US missile interceptor systems, and those with Bulgaria and Romania for new bases, not only represent a threat to Europe's sovereignty, but create a real risk of new confrontation in Europe.

The withdrawal from Iraq and Afghanistan of NATO troops and the Western coalition led by the United States is necessary. The international community as well as the European Union must support Afghanistan's population in finding a political solution through non-military ways on the basis of respect of international law and human rights. As further measures we demand the closing of all NATO and US bases in Europe. We are against the US (or any European) Satellite Defence Installations with European and non-European deployments, and fully support the Czech, Polish, Bulgarian and Romanian citizens who fight against them. We reject any military misuse of the European Galileo System.

The development and trade policies of the European Union must meet the Millennium Development Goals in reality, and must realign to the principle of equality of all countries. The bilateral European Partnership Agreements are the wrong way. The international trade policy of the European Union is to be measured by giving adequate answers for solving global social and ecological problems. The fight against growing global poverty and imbalances must be the focus of development co-operation – the misuse of development co-operation for continuing a kind of colonial relations, for the one-sided support of export industries in favour of European enterprises, or as a geopolitical instrument must be stopped. We want a ban on the transformation of food into fuel. We demand debt redemption for the poorest countries of the world, and revision of the structural adjustment programmes of the World Bank and the International Monetary Fund.

We support a further development of Mediterranean co-operation. It is the key for achieving peace and security in the Middle East. We need the active participation of all political forces and civil societies in the countries involved. A democratic and transparent process must bridge the gap between countries to the North and South of the Mediterranean. This is the only way to avoid turning the ambitious political project of the Mediterranean Union into a political structure of inequality.

A Mediterranean of lasting and stable peace is impossible without solving the conflict in the Middle East. The essential precondition for that is recognising and realising the right of the Palestinian people to have an independent, viable state side by side with the state of Israel – with equal rights and living together in a peaceful neighbourhood. The European Left will do its utmost to demand and push the European Union and its member countries to act consistently in that direction. Europe needs to emancipate itself from the US 'Greater Middle East' plan, to engage itself actively for an end of the military occupation of the Palestinian territories, for the removal of the 'Wall', in accordance with the Advisory Opinion of the International Court of Justice, and for the strict fulfilment of all corresponding UN resolutions. The European Union must take more political steps to request the support of the Arab countries in the region, and to stimulate the growing awareness of civil societies working towards an active conflict-solving policy.

The European Left rejects the confrontational course of US and

EU policies towards Iran – in particular, regarding a solution to the conflict about nuclear energy – and demands strict political negotiations. The European Left expresses its solidarity with political and social forces striving for the consistent implementation and guarantee of human rights in Iran.

The European Left stresses its commitment to a process of security and co-operation of all states in the Mediterranean and Middle East region(s), including the right of the Sahrawi people to self-determination on the basis of the existing UN-resolutions 1754 and 1783.

Turkey must respect in a legally binding way the political and human rights of all people living in the country, including all minorities. It must carry out social and legal reforms in accordance with the rule of law to pave a democratic and peaceful way for all Kurdish citizens in Turkey. This will also contribute to a political solution for the Kurdish people in other countries of the Middle East.

Significant movement on the Cyprus problem, and the change of climate after the election of Dimitris Christofias to the presidency of the Republic, opens up new hopeful prospects regarding efforts for the reunification of the island. The conduct of official negotiations between the leaders of the two communities under UN auspices should lead to a bi-zonal, bi-communal federal solution with political equality, as stated in the relevant UN Resolutions, and on the basis of High-Level Agreements, international and European law.

The European Left favours the creation of all political and economic conditions for peaceful co-existence of European peoples and states. Europe needs an economic and social space which does not exclude any European country, and which is based on a varied bi- and multilateral system of agreements. The European Left stands for the further enlargement of the European Union, and for a stable, all-European structure to overcome political and economic divisions that still exist in Europe. With that in mind, the European Left supports, in particular, the preservation of democratic governance, guaranteeing and realizing human rights for all people in daily practice, and respecting and protecting minorities and the state of law as important preconditions for negotiating with countries applying for EU membership. The European Union itself must be made ready, politically and economically, for further enlargement as well.

The European Left demands the consistent implementation of the EU's new neighbourhood policy on the basis of equality, in particular with regard to countries of the Commmonwealth of Independent States and the Western Balkan states.

IV
A democratic and equal Europe

The democratic reconstruction of Europe remains an urgent task for today.

All human beings living in European Union member states have the right to participate in shaping the Union and its future development, whether born here or not. The European Union must open up to the democratic participation of all its people, or it will have no future.

We stand for the strengthening of individual rights and freedoms, as well as the fundamental social and political rights of all people living in the European Union. The Charter of Fundamental Rights must become legally binding, and be developed further. The European Union should join the European Court of Human Rights Charter. The European Left stands for guaranteeing the full equality of women and men in all aspects of life. We strive for a European regulation guaranteeing a woman's right to decide about her body, free contraception, and abortion within the public health system. We promote European regulations criminalising any gender violence. Sufficient material and personal resources are to be provided to all victims of such violence.

The European Union must protect and promote the rights of those discriminated against because of their ethnic origin, sexual orientation and gender identity, religion, ideology, disability, and age. We demand the respect of all minority rights and consistent action against racism, xenophobia, ultra-nationalism, chauvinism, fascism, anti-communism, homophobia, and any other form of discrimination. We are in favour of a secular Europe in the sense that all the states' policies should be secular.

The Europe we want needs a democratisation of the economy. Coalition, co-determination and the right to strike must apply across borders. We reject the subordination of social and Trade Union standards to the basic freedoms of the single market, as ruled by the European Court of Justice. On the contrary: the rights and opportunities for working people to participate in management decisions, for example concerning investments or production regulation, must be enlarged and fixed by law.

The European Left stands for a cultural policy of the European Union based on intercultural dialogue and education. It resists the unlimited liberalisation of cultural services. We want a dialogue of the cultures to become a pacifist policy principle at local and European levels. We support the UNESCO Convention on the Protection and Promotion of the Diversity of Cultural Expressions, in which the preservation and promotion of the diversity of regional cultures is binding under international law.

We also demand a transparent media policy. The sources of economic productivity, cultural hegemony, and political as well as military power are increasingly dependent on the production, storage and conversion of information and knowledge. Therefore, access to societies' communications and information, and their acquisition, are essential issues of democratic participation at both national and European levels. Furthermore, the democratisation of production, treatment and appropriation of information and knowledge is inevitably needed to challenge digital capitalism. We are in favour of democratic structures of public service media, with cheap and easy access to modern cultural arenas such as the internet, and free codes and programming without the unlawful use of social networks and personal data.

It is necessary to reverse the Bologna Process, the subordination of the school, university and research needs to the interests of private industries, the profit-makers of the free market. Education is a human right. We support all movements of students, parents and teachers in Europe who oppose the Bologna reforms and defend, regardless of the country, a public and free education.

European public education needs be rooted in the principles and values defining the essential features of European culture. School must be, in all member states, a meeting place free of confrontation among cultures co-existing in an ever more multi-cultural and multi-religious society, as a necessary premiss of the authentic development of an education in peace and gender equality. At the same time, universities need to be able to develop their prominent role of cultural and scientific training, unlinked to the logic of the market.

To reclaim the political space in the European Union for all people living here, the European Parliament must be given the power of legislative initiative. Direct participation in European decision making, such as the Citizen-Agora introduced by the European Parliament, including referenda at European Union and national levels on EU landmark decisions, must be possible. The European Union institutions (Council, Commission and Parliament) must open up to the participation of civil societies, who should have the possibility to control their decisions. The European Union-wide anti-terror measures and laws are to be abandoned. We want the abolition of the European Union's list of 'terrorist organizations', which jeopardises our freedom.

We want a cosmopolitan Europe open to migration. Not Europe as a fortress, which repels people in need. A common European Union refugee and migration policy, in accordance with the Geneva Convention, is needed. People who flee from persecution because of their political commitment, ideology, religion, or sexual orientation must find protection and asylum in Europe. We demand the recognition of gender-related and non-governmental persecution as grounds for asylum, and call for the specific protection of child refugees. Therefore, we reject the already existing FRONTEX-system of border control, and demand the rejection of all plans on the implementation of the 'Pact on Migration and Asylum' and the 'Returns Directive'. Detention prisons must be closed.

We oppose the choices of European Union and European governments, which impose mechanisms of 'preventive repression' and 'preventive filing of personal data (Prüm Treaty)', create suspects, and offer the judicial and police forces, private companies, every interested state, even the secret services, the right to use personal data through the biggest existing data base, under the pretext of defence of public safety.

We, the parties of the European Left, campaign together and in our countries for these goals in the run-up to the 2009 elections to the European Parliament. We want a strong left parliamentary group in order to be able to change Europe. Each vote for a candidate of the European Left is a vote for a peaceful, social, ecological, democratic and feminist Europe, living in solidarity!

Take your chance, change Europe now!

Berlin, 29 November 2008

Source: http://www.european-left.org/english/news/electoral_platform/

Also available from Socialist Renewal

New Labour's Attack on Public Services - *by Dexter Whitfield*

New Labour is creating markets in public services on an unprecedented scale. Action by alliances of trade unions, community organisations and civil society organisations is urgently required to protect education, health and other vital public provision.

Price: £11.99 | ISBN: 0 85124 725 3

Nuclear Reactors: Do we need more? - *by Christopher Gifford*

The case for 'fast-tracking' new nuclear reactors has not been made, argues an experienced health and safety inspector who has probed nuclear's safety record.

Price: £2.00 | ISBN: 0 85124 154 9

The Social Europe We Need
by Robin Blackburn, André Brie MEP, Ken Coates, Christina Beatty & Stephen Fothergill

The European Union is, at present, the only global entity with an economic weight & political potential equal to that of the United States. We should ensure that Europe represents a different social model to that of the United States, instead of becoming more like it.

Price: £9.99 | ISBN: 0 85124 703 2

Railtracks in the Sky: Air Transport Deregulation and the Competitive Market - *by Peter Reed*

An International *managed* regime for air transport could be made to work, starting at the European Union level.

Price: £9.99 | ISBN: 0 85124 671 0

Physician Heal Thyself - The NHS needs a voice of its own
by Duncan Smith

An NHS Staff College would allow directions from the top to be complemented by feedback from below. The NHS' former Chief Training Officer outlines the case.

Price: £3.00| ISBN: 0 85124 667 2

The Captive Local State: Local Democracy under Seige
by Peter Latham

What is happening to local councils? The author, Secretary of the Labour Campaign for Open Local Government, analyses the changes under New Labour.

Price: £2.00 | ISBN: 0 85124 651 6

Safety First? Did the Health & Safety Commission do its job?
by Christopher Gifford

"This pamphlet is about how opportunities to protect people from abuse were taken or missed in the 25 year history of the Health & Safety Commission."

Price: £2.00 | ISBN: 0 85124 652 4

Spokesman Books, Russell House, Bulwell Lane, Nottingham, NG6 0BT
Email: elfeuro@compuserve.com | Tel: 0115 970 8381 | Fax: 0115 942 0433

www.spokesmanbooks.com

—— ALSO AVAILABLE ——

Workers' Control
Another world is possible

Arguments from the **Institute for Workers' Control**
by **KEN COATES**
Contributions by **DEREK SIMPSON & TONY WOODLEY**

‟This book is a significant contribution to the ongoing discussion around issues of workers' control. We believe that this selection of writings will assist in the huge tasks facing us today, namely expanding trade union organisation, strengthening collective bargaining and reasserting and developing workers' control over their lives and industry."

Jeremy Dear *National Union of Journalists*
Andy Gilchrist *Fire Brigades Union*
Billy Hayes *Communication Workers' Union*
Joe Marino *Bakers, Food & Allied Workers' Union*
Mick Rix *Associated Society of Locomotive Engineers & Firemen*
Mark Serwotka *Public & Commercial Services Union*
Tony Woodley *Transport & General Workers' Union*

£7.99   www.spokesmanbooks.com

THE SPOKESMAN
Founded by Bertrand Russell

Slump and War

Edited by **Ken Coates**

Meltdown Election - **Noam Chomsky**
South Ossetia - **Roy and Zhores Medvedev**
From A to X - **John Berger**
Weapons for Pensions - **Richard Minns**
The Crisis - **Oskar Lafontaine**
Edward Carpenter, Unsung Hero
Michael Barratt Brown
Reviews:
Chris Gifford - Sick Planet
John Daniels - Economics for Everyone
Stan Newens - TomDispatch
Tony Simpson - John le Carré
Henry McCubbin - Spin Europe
Peter Jackson - Wilfred Burchett

£6.00   Issue 102

Slump and War

Tskhinvali: Shock & Awe

Edited by **Ken Coates**

America's Role in Georgia - **Vladimir Putin**
In Praise of the High Shadow
Mahmoud Darwish, Saifedean Ammous
New American Cold War - **Stephen Cohen**
Intelligence Disgrace - **Andrew Mackinlay** MP
Punishing the Innocent - **Gareth Peirce**
interviewed by **Moazzam Begg**
Mohammad - **Mahmoud Darwish**
Nothing for the Hungry - **Jean Ziegler**
Roots of Hunger - **James Petras**
From Judgment to Calculation - **Mike Cooley**
Revisiting Tom Paine - **Trevor Griffiths**
Issue 101 *interviewed by* **Ann Talbot**   £6.00

Tskhinvali
Shock and Awe

Subscription to ***The Spokesman*** (4 issues) costs £20 (£25 ex UK)
Spokesman Books, Russell House, Nottingham, NG6 0BT, England
Tel: 0115 9708318 - Fax: 0115 9420433 - elfeuro@compuserve.com
Order online at www.spokesmanbooks.com

"I've just had a chance to read *The Spokesman*... it's really first-rate." **Noam Chomsky**